MOMENT TIME™
PLAYER/COACH MARKETING

The S.Y.S.T.E.M.
Know, Choose, Grow,
and Give Yourself to
Creating Your Direct Sales
Dream Team

CLIFFORD TODD

BookWise
publishing

Moment Time™ **Player/Coach Marketing**
Clifford Todd
Copyright © 2018 Clifford Todd. All Rights Reserved.

The *Moment Time*™ trademark is the property of Clifford Todd.
Intrinsic Validation is a key concept owned and taught by
the Og Mandino Leadership Institute.
Habit Finder™ is a trade name belonging to The Og Group.

No part of this book may be reproduced or transmitted in any form by any means, electronic or mechanical, including photocopying, recording or by any information storage and retrieval system, without specific written permission from the publisher or author. The scanning, uploading, and distribution of this book via the Internet or via any other means without the permission of the publisher or author is illegal and punishable by law. Please purchase only authorized electronic editions, and do not participate in or encourage electronic piracy of copyrighted materials.

BookWise Publishing, LLC • www.bookwisepublishing.com
Book Cover and Interior Design by Francine Eden Platt
Eden Graphics, Inc. • www.edengraphics.net

Library of Congress Control Number: Pending
ISBN #978-1-60645-228-8
Paperback $14.97

10 9 8 7 6 5 4 3 2 1
Printed in the USA

Version 8 16 2018

TABLE OF CONTENTS

Dedication iv
Freedoms You Will Enjoy. 1
Why and How to Use This Book 3
I. Friending (Context for Phase 1, Scouting). 8
II. Clarifying 13
III. Trusting. 15
IV. Inviting (Context for Phase 2, Training Camp) 18
V. Joining 21
VI. Player/Coaching. 23
VII. Unforgettable, Infallible, Unstoppable 26
VIII. Manage Your Freedom Expectations 30
IX. Ongoing Learning. 33
X. Ultimate: Go Even Deeper 40
Meet the Author, Clifford Todd 43
Resources 45
Postscript 46

Mastering others is **STRENGTH.**
Mastering yourself is **TRUE POWER.**
— *Lao Tzu*

DEDICATION

To **Og Mandino, Robert S. Hartman, and Dave Blanchard**.

These men are responsible for my being able to Og-ment my life and responsibly bring this work forward in my efforts to transform the network marketing industry.

To **Elle J. Bennett**

Elle bravely co-authored her story in *Moment Time*™ *Connections*. We sat next to each other while she was flying to Australia to see her parents. Og Mandino is her father's favorite author. We told her story to show flight crews how to create income during idle ground time.

To **Jeffrey Van Dyk**

Jeffrey taught me Tribal Story Marketing, or how to use our "wounds" to connect with our tribes. Happily, we have known each other for ten years, and I finally accepted and declared myself as the thought leader willing to risk challenging the fifty years of habitual training this industry has endured.

To **Hawley Todd,** TSSF, Executive Director, Episcopal Healing Ministries

Hawley is the sibling who helped me process my Jeffrey-wounding stories and who made sure I had sufficient funding to transition from writing on an ancient 2011 Mac Book to completing this third book starring *Moment Time*™.

Thank you all for helping me enjoy living and accepting my intrinsic worth as a human being.

FREEDOMS YOU WILL ENJOY

1. **TIME & FINANCIAL FREEDOM**
2. **EMOTIONAL & MENTAL FREEDOM**

Go confidently in the direction of your dreams.
Live the life you have imagined.

– Henry David Thoreau

July 4, 2018. Independence Day. I'm making my own declaration today, honoring our American freedoms.

People seek time and financial freedom. It's a basic human want. Unfortunately, as Thoreau also said, "Men lead lives of quiet desperation."

Just how bad is it? The vast majority (87%) of employees spend half their waking hours uninspired by their work, working for people not likely to acknowledge their worth.

According to Gallup data published by the *Washington Post*, most employees (63%) are "not engaged," not motivated, and unlikely to exert extra effort in their jobs. Worse, 24% of employees in data from 140 countries are "actively *disengaged*" or truly unhappy and unproductive. Only 13% are "engaged" in their jobs, emotionally invested in their work, and focused on helping their organizations improve.

If you are an aspiring entrepreneur, this book is for you. If you are currently employed, this book encourages you to access your money that does not show up in your take-home pay. You can increase your next paycheck. This book encourages you to develop meaningful relationships that will enrich your and others' lives. And within a matter of months, not years, it can guide your journey into time and financial freedom.

What do time and financial freedom mean to you? Would working twenty hours a week satisfy you? Would you prefer one week per month leisurely traveling?

How much income would you like to earn? Do you enjoy simple pleasures, or do you prefer luxuries? How much income is enough, or is more income never enough?

Only you can answer these questions for you.

What do emotional and mental freedom mean? Are you working just to survive? Do you feel free to live how you want to?

If you are not satisfied with how your life is turning out, you have incalculable value waiting for you by following the S.Y.S.T.E.M. described within these pages. You are the only one who will see its value exactly the way you do.

Why? You are the only one who can Know Yourself, Choose Yourself, Grow Yourself, and Give Yourself to creating your direct sales dream team—the team that will deliver the time and financial freedom you desire.

July 4, 1776. The Founding Fathers declared our country's Independence. If you desire time and financial freedom, living consistent with your values, and experiencing peace of mind, the solutions in this book will work for you.

May you experience joy as we journey together.

WHY AND HOW TO USE THIS BOOK

The real voyage of discovery consists not in seeking new landscapes, but in having new eyes.

– Marcel Proust

In centuries past sailors longed for a map to the distant lands of their dreams. My grandmother traced our ancestry back to the days of Erik the Red. Courageous sailors would sail west until they had consumed half of their food and water. Then they would return home. Family stories include Erik's father telling his grandson, Leif Eriksson, *"Keep going. You won't run out of resources."* I've dreamed being a 20-something great grandson…

This book is today's map. It invites you to safely seek your dreams and live joyfully free. This book focuses on applying the people connection skills (the tip of the iceberg) as described in my companion book *Moment Time™ Rests on the Habit Finder*.

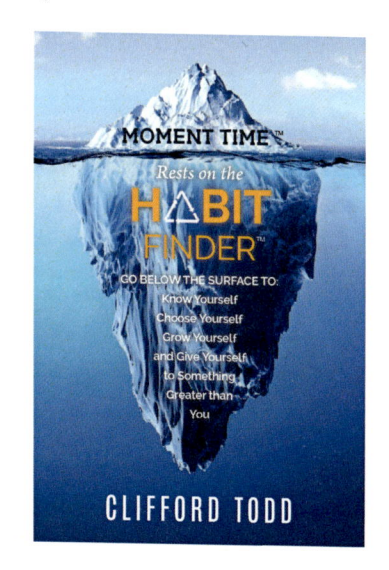

Og Mandino, in his legendary classic, *The Greatest Salesman in the World*, expressed the wisdom shared with Leif as **"I will act now."**

Ironically, breakneck speed is counter-productive.

Two phrases you will hear often: **Slow is fast. Less is more.** Nature never acts in haste. You are an evolving human being. Will you take charge of your evolution, or will you allow your current habits to enslave your future?

Og maintains the difference between those who fail and those who succeed lies in the difference in their habits. Good habits are the key to all success. Bad habits are the unlocked door to failure. Og says we will form good habits and become their slave. I say, "practice people connecting skills until you can't do them wrong." Same message, different words.

Before we get deeply into this book, I'd like to share a little bit about me, so we aren't complete strangers as well as why you should listen.

My first job out of graduate school was to become the first economist for the American Medical Association. For the last 46 years, I've been self-employed focusing on medical care/health care.

In 1972 I joined (part-time) Holiday Magic, a network marketing company. I latched onto its promises of time and money freedom only to lose $12,000. I tried company after company, and finally made it big in Nikken during 1991. My third month check was $26,118. My highest single check from any network marketing company was $61,324 in 2004.

Fast forward to 2016. I was recovering from two painful network marketing failures. You may relate to *"I'll never do this frickin' business again."* Releasing a forty-year alcohol habit led to my writing a network marketing book that led to my becoming an Og Mandino Leadership Coach. On this Fourth of July, I started writing *my* declaration of independence, using my system with the wisdom I've gained while coaching the Og Mandino Leadership Practicum.

Moment Time™ *Player/Coach Marketing* is a map to time and financial freedom and a S.Y.S.T.E.M., an acronym for *Save Yourself Significant Time, Energy & Money*. It's not a short-cut; it's just the fastest, easiest, and safest route.

My friend and fellow Og Coach, Ken Kovach, refers to me as a "Sherpa guide," similar to the sure-footed mountain man who has the skill to lead you safely up a jagged mountain trail. Jagged is indeed an apt description for network marketing.

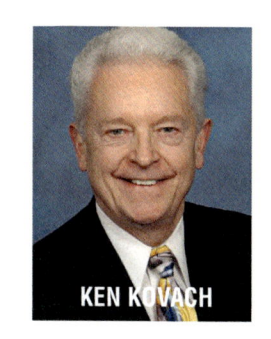

KEN KOVACH

Historically, network marketing is a pain-inducing industry. A few tenths of one percent of those who enter the industry earn over fifty percent of all income paid to representatives. The other 996+ out of 1,000 people buy the dream of time and income freedom only to fail, their dreams shattered. I know this pain. I failed for 20 years before my first six-figure success. And I've failed a few times since.

What's important is where we are now and where we want to go.

When people ask what I do, I respond, "Aspiring entrepreneurs and their coaches hire me to uplevel their people connection skills, so that they attract only heart-centered, passionate, business saavy team members and clients, even if they shy away from direct sales. At the end of the day, they have fun meeting people and reconnecting with old friends without mentioning products or business opportunities. In less than five hours a week, they determine who the one person is *that week* who would be best served by having a conversation about playing one of our teams. These one-conversation-a-week moments lead to time and financial freedom within seven to nine months."

Employers make my work easy. They pay people enough to keep them working, and employees work hard enough not to get fired. To feel joyously alive and happy about how their lives are turning out, people must *hire themselves and start their own businesses.*

Fact: that "being in business for yourself is the best personal development course in the world."

I call my system **Player/Coach Marketing.** The old model for network marketing has carried negative stigma and drawn intense negative reactions for five decades, with good reason. By most standards, 98-plus % of the 20-plus million current U.S. distributors will ultimately fail, if they don't quit first. Sad, but true.

The critical distinction of *Player/Coach Marketing* lies in what people do. The old model is to tell everyone about your product or opportunity. That's vomiting information. In the new model, **people build engaged teams who play and coach simultaneously.** In simple terms, they focus 95-plus % of their effort on **team building.** Technology and social media trigger product sales. Team members learn how to enjoy their lives and feel better about themselves while they create time and financial freedom.

Corporate America spends millions to find the right executives, based on their competence, character, capability, reliability, determination, and loyalty. The desired result? Hire the best executive from among the best candidates.

Moment Time™ is a leader identifier system akin to the multiple interviews that executive candidates endure. And ethically, it's under the radar as a highly effective player identification process.

The "**Sherpa Rules**" for keeping the player identification process ethical center on human *being*, not human *doing*.

1. **Concentrate** on just being present in the NOW.
2. **It's all about *them*.** Park your personal agenda before you engage in face-to-face contact.
3. **Focus your awareness.** Breathe. A five-second meditation following your breath does wonders. A 2011 study published by Harvard cites why meditation enhances your empathy for others.
4. **Listen to your intuition.** Listen for inspiration.
5. **Ask, don't tell.** Probe deeper into knowing the person in front of you When words come out of your friend's mouth, *they* accept what they say as true. When you tell them the *same* thing, they most likely will doubt it.
6. **Share a personal story** about how the two of you share similar experiences, not about products or services. Weave it in; don't just jump in.
7. **Goals:** *first*, serve the person you're with. Aim to leave the new friend better off than when you met. *Second*, discern if this is this someone you want to invite to the next moment? Or is this someone you want to invite to become a social media friend?
8. **Discern**, then trust your intuition as to what's next.

Information does not change people. *People change people*. The best way to grow into being the best you can be is to practice the *Moment Time*™ moments. Continue practicing, and you will get better and better.

I

FRIENDING

(Context for Phase 1, Scouting)

To see things in the seed, this is genius.

– Lao Tzu

Friending is meeting someone new or reconnecting with an old friend. Most things in our lives are based on our relationships with people.

Friending is the first moment of a six-moment S.Y.S.T.E.M. (*Save Yourself Significant Time, Energy & Money*). The system has two phases: Scouting and Training Camp. Sports analogies make the concepts easier to understand. **Player/Coach Marketing** emulates professional sports. Send scouts to watch college players play. Invite the good ones to Training Camp. During try-outs, keep some players, cut the rest.

If this sounds brutal, remember the Sherpa Rules. During Phase 1, Scouting, you are simply collecting friends, being of service to them in an ethical manner. Building new friendships take time. *Slow is fast. Less is more.* Phase 1 has three moments: *Friending, Clarifying, and Trusting*. In functional terms, you notice what's important to the new friend; you understand them by asking about their dreams and challenges; and you let them know they are understood by discussing their plans to achieve their dreams.

When has a new friend ever invested the time to really get to know you, to know what's important to you, and offered to listen and help you achieve what's important to you?

If you have ever had this experience, is this person *unforgettable*? Is this person still your friend? If yes, you already know that the Scouting Phase is all about creating life-long relationships/friends.

Happily, some of these new friends will ultimately join your business, but only after you invite them into your world, and they accept your invitation to listen.

With some new friends and reconnected old friends, you will discover ways to mutually enrich each other's lives.

Either way, everyone wins. I like that, and you will, too.

The System cycles in two-week segments. *Friending* involves meeting one new person, or reconnecting with an old friend, six days per week, or 12 people every two weeks.

THE BEST WAY TO PREDICT THE FUTURE IS TO CREATE IT.

— PETER DRUCKER

SCOUTING

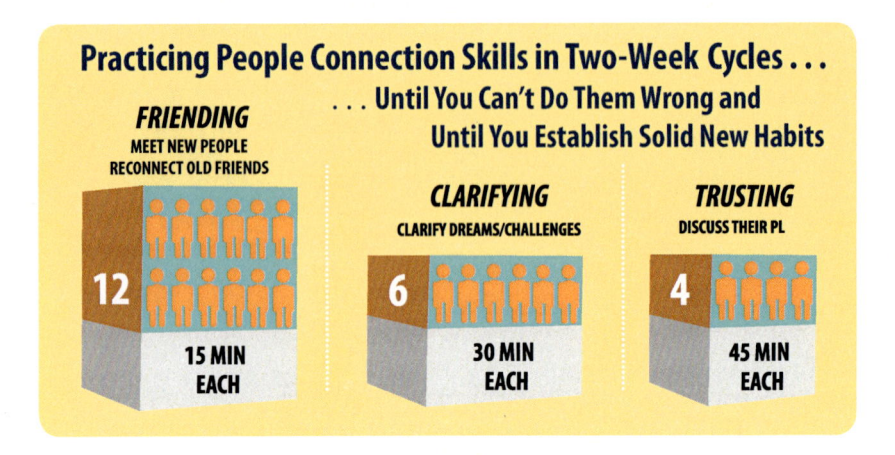

Practicing People Connection Skills in Two-Week Cycles...
... Until You Can't Do Them Wrong and Until You Establish Solid New Habits

FRIENDING
MEET NEW PEOPLE
RECONNECT OLD FRIENDS
12 — 15 MIN EACH

CLARIFYING
CLARIFY DREAMS/CHALLENGES
6 — 30 MIN EACH

TRUSTING
DISCUSS THEIR PL
4 — 45 MIN EACH

KNOW YOURSELF: THE FIRST CORE VALUE

Let's get tactical. General George S. Patton wisdom: engage where you have a strategic advantage. Hang out where the people you want to meet hang out, particularly if it involves doing something you enjoy. Hanging-out time is important. You want the person you want to engage to feel comfortable talking for a few minutes. My goal is to engage someone new for about 15 minutes.

My favorite places involve exercise (hot yoga, strength training, and Silver Sneaker gyms), networking meetings, even church. Church works because I park my agenda and never violate church sanctity. If you've been approached by an insurance salesman at church, you know what I mean.

A great way to initiate connecting with people is described in *The Greatest Salesman in the World*.

"And how will I confront each whom I meet? In only one way. In silence, and to myself, I will address him and say I Love You. Though spoken in silence, these

words will shine in my eyes, unwrinkle my brow, bring a smile to my lips, and echo in my voice, and his heart will be opened."

In neuro-science terms, mirror neurons in others' brains pick up and accurately interpret the energy our mirror neurons release. Wikipedia defines it this way: "A mirror neuron is a neuron that fires both when an animal acts and when the animal observes the same action performed by another, thus the neuron mirrors the behavior of the other, as though the observer were itself acting."

We can connect with others and deepen these connections before words are ever spoken. When we send out in silence the Og-inspired, "I love you," the recipients feel it and send it back to us.

Imagine hanging out at a favorite place, sending out loving energy. Your mirror neuron radar will tell you whom to approach and whom to stay away from. When in doubt, retest it. This unconscious radar will keep you from engaging with people who are not open to mutually serving.

Once you connect with words, the *first* task is to notice what's important to the other person and say what you notice. In saying so, you validate the uniqueness of the person. Implicitly, you acknowledge that person's human worth. At OsteoStrong, I noticed that my friend Sarah Glicken, has her Mom's handwriting tattooed on her wrist. That simple act of noticing and saying so led to our becoming real friends.

CLIFFORD TODD

By the way, if you live in Los Angeles, check out Sarah's strength conditioning center in Mar Vista. My functionality (body strength, bone density and balance) has increased by 63% in nine sessions. Sarah and her partner Robert can be reached at **(424) 331-1404**. Mention my name. They will arrange two complimentary visits for you. Robert is a veteran who, now in his 50's, is in the best shape of his life. Robert is coaching me so that on December 1, 2018, I will be in my best shape since my college wrestling days. I'll be 75 years old!!! Robert is an appreciated Player/Coach in my life.

The *second* task is to discern if you want to set up a second moment with this person or just establish ongoing contact via social media. My friend and Habit Finder Coach, Jessica Faltot, recommends asking yourself, *"Is this person heart-centered?"* If yes, set up a time to meet again.

Set appointments while face-to-face. Two to three days later for the next moment appointment is preferable.

If no, establish continuing contact via social media.

The more you connect with other people, the more you will reveal to yourself your own true worth. You will dive deeper and deeper into living fully human. You will begin being more joyously alive by ***knowing yourself***.

Every moment is an opportunity to be more aware of who you are.

– Bill Harris

II

CLARIFYING

CHOOSE YOURSELF: THE SECOND CORE VALUE

Clarifying, the second moment of *Moment Time*™, is a longer conversation where you ask the person to talk about their dreams, what they want to create in their lives, and the challenges they are facing. If you ever did a pre-teen sleepover, this moment is similar to the two of you under the covers with a flashlight, talking into the night about what your lives will be like when you grow up.

Tactically, the **Sherpa Rules** still apply. ***You are a human being (not a human doing) fully present, aware, in service of the person you are meeting for the second time.***

Tactically, we have three more Sherpa-rules:

1. If you were able to easily talk at the first location, go to the same place. Your friend enjoys going there, so they already has good vibes going there.

2. Arrive early. Demonstrate respect—arrive first.

3. Make a show of turning off your cell phone. I like to say, "I'm here with you. Not my cellphone."

People want to be validated for how they contribute to others, to their families, and to themselves. *Clarifying* is powerful when others feel you understand them. They *will* feel you understand when you ask about their wants, whys, and challenges **without trying to fix them.**

How do you keep people talking about themselves? Sometimes, it's a simple, *"Tell me more about that,"* or *"If you had that, what else would that do for you?"*

Slow is fast. *Clarifying* conversations average about thirty minutes. Six moments every two weeks involve three hours; an hour and a half a week.

When I am in Clarifying conversations, I look for two things. Is this person passion-driven? What pain does this person feel? **(And if possible, how acute is the pain?)**

Scott Quinney, an Og Coach and mountain biker, gives this clue to discern if you're talking with passion-driven people: "Look at their posture. Body language speaks louder than words and tells fewer lies."

Experts say that human communication relies 55% on body language, 38% on tone of voice, and 7% on the words spoken. I find this particularly true when people talk about their pain. The more a person fidgets or squirms, the more connected they are to their pain.

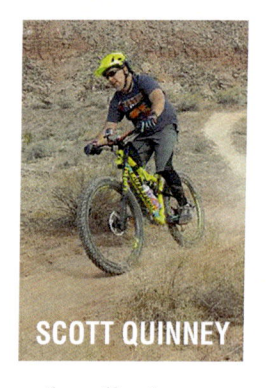

As you practice *Clarifying*, you will gain new insights into the characteristics you want in teammates. Keep this top-of-mind: *Teamwork makes the Dream work.*

As you practice, you will also gain insights into what you want your life to become. You will be **Choosing Yourself.**

III

TRUSTING

GROW YOURSELF: THE THIRD CORE VALUE

The transition to the third moment, *Trusting,* is as simple as saying, "I'm enjoying hearing what you're saying. Would you like to sit down over coffee or lunch and brainstorm your plans to achieve what you want? I'd be happy to listen, and perhaps I can even offer an idea or two?"

Once people agree to brainstorm their ideas for achieving what they want, they are exhibiting an entrepreneurial trait—*the capacity for passion-driven action.*

The people-connection goal for *Trusting* moments is for your new friends or reconnected friends to feel understood. **Fact: feeling understood is the greatest gift we can give.**

Slow is fast. The average *Trusting* moment is 45 minutes. Four Trusting moments every two weeks take about three hours; about an hour and a half per week.

During *Trusting* moments, set aside your agenda, show up early, be present and aware, and serve friends by helping them make sound decisions. You will best serve yourself and your friends when you imagine being a venture capitalist reviewing your friend's business plan. The basics of a good business plan are:

1. Their **goals**, what they want to achieve, by when;
2. The **strategies** to achieve those goals;
3. The necessary **resources** to execute the plan;
4. A favorable **business environment**;
5. The right **tactics** within their chosen field;
6. A **personal environment** to support their efforts;
7. And the **WILL TO WIN**.

As you review the basics of their business plans, you will establish unequivocally that you understand what's important to your friends. *They will feel understood.*

How deeply do you take these conversations? Deep enough to engender trust to link your lives together. You have a responsibility to keep the conversation centered on *their* plans and what works for *them*. It's not about you.

As a minimum, you and your friends, one at a time, can openly address these trust questions:

1. Do your friends trust their ability to plan their business?
2. Do your friends trust themselves enough to hire themselves to run their business?
3. Do your friends trust you enough to respect your guidance?
4. Do you trust your friends enough to help them guide their business for months/years to come?

When you show up and position yourself as coming from an unattached service state, you will completely dissolve the natural and innate resistances we all have as human beings.

The Og Mandino Leadership Institute calls this "Lowering the Walls of Resistance." How valuable is dissolving this resistance? The Hartman Institute estimates in non-adversarial relationships that *honoring others' human value releases an additional 40% of productive energy from the people validated.*

Imagine how much better your life and their lives will be once you begin validating everyone in your life, not once, but regularly. In doing so, you will **Grow Yourself.**

Tell me sufficiently why I should do something, and I will move heaven and earth to do it.

– Socrates

The QUALITY of a person's life is directly proportional to their dedication to EXCELLENCE, regardless of their chosen field of endeavor.

- VINCE LOMBARDI

IV

INVITING

(Context for Phase 2, Training Camp)

A good plan executed quickly is far better than the best plan executed too late.

– General George S. Patton

The Scouting Phase moments, *Friending, Clarifying,* and *Trusting,* center on observing your new friends or reconnected old friends and discerning whom you want to invite to try out for your direct sales team. Keep the invitation simple:

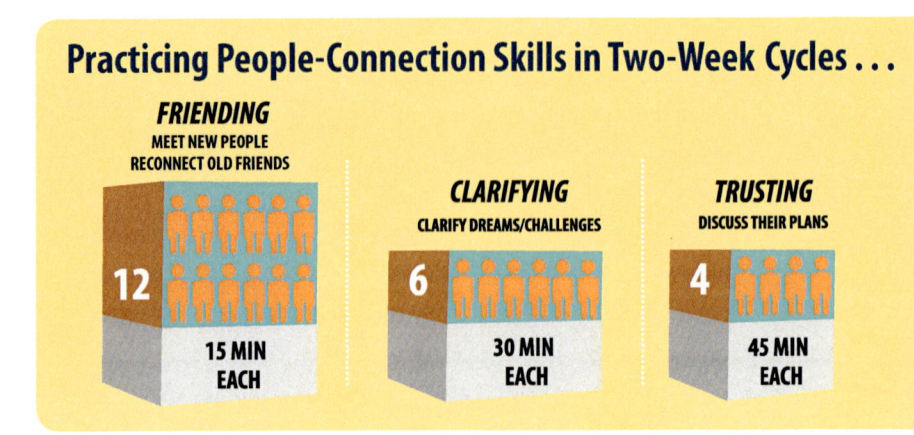

Practicing People-Connection Skills in Two-Week Cycles . . .

FRIENDING
MEET NEW PEOPLE
RECONNECT OLD FRIENDS
12 — 15 MIN EACH

CLARIFYING
CLARIFY DREAMS/CHALLENGES
6 — 30 MIN EACH

TRUSTING
DISCUSS THEIR PLANS
4 — 45 MIN EACH

"Would you be willing to step into my world, and let my Player/Coach and I share a little bit about our industry and why we chose it to achieve our dreams?"

The graphic below repeats the scouting moments and shows the three Training Camp moments. *Inviting* is the first conversation. Only two people every two weeks try out.

You always win: Moments of time invested scouting eliminate enrolling people on your team who will later suck up time and energy but will most likely never build their own team.

People often ask, *"In simple terms, what exactly do I do?"*

Just be you. Talk with people. When people qualify through the three scouting conversations, and you feel it's in the best interest for both of you, invite them to step into your world. Introduce your Player/Coach and friend to each other. Have the enrollment conversation called *Inviting*. Just listen. Your Player/Coach will lead the Inviting conversations. If we choose to work together, I will be your Player/Coach.

In time, you will learn how to Player/Coach your team. But let's not get ahead of ourselves.

...Until You Can't Do Them Wrong and Until You Establish Solid New Habits

INVITING	JOINING	PLAYER/COACHING
ENROLLMENT CONVERSATION	MUTUAL COMMITMENT	CONTINUOUS IMPROVEMENT
2 — TIME VARIES	1 — TIME VARIES	ON-GOING

All direct sales companies reward a Player's building a team. The critical distinction is *how* each company rewards those behaviors. Over the last 46 years, I've listened to dozens of company executives boast about their compensation plans. I know what makes achieving time and financial freedom easier or harder. I'll answer your questions about specific plans. It's that important.

What's fun in the system graphic is seeing how only one conversation per week is invested in inviting people to join your team. What's extraordinary are benefits derived from interacting with people not invited to *Inviting* moments.

You will build new mutually enriching friendships (just like I did at OsteoStrong). In multiple ways, you continuously **Grow Yourself.**

> Happiness cannot be traveled to, owned, earned, worn, or consumed. Happiness is the spiritual experience of living every minute with love, grace, and gratitude.
>
> – DENIS WAITLEY

V

JOINING

GIVE YOURSELF: THE FOURTH CORE VALUE

The mission of *Moment Time*™ is for you to trust the core value process: Know Yourself. Choose Yourself. Grow Yourself. And Give Yourself to something greater than you.

In *Moment Time*™, the fifth moment is *Joining*—the moment when two people mutually make the choice and the commitment to work together. Dave Blanchard witnessed this in the Japanese culture. *An older, calmer wise one accepts the responsibility to train a younger, eager seeker. The younger one pledges his best efforts to listen, learn, and integrate the ways of the wiser one into his daily practices.*

The younger one's commitment to follow the wise one's ways is his or her journey into a state of joy.

Do you see the word *Joy* inside the letters of *Journey*? It's fascinating when we see, hear, feel, taste, and experience being *present*. The Journey starts and ends in Joy.

Emotionally intelligent people live in the NOW and find joy and fulfillment in all they do. They manage the inevitable gaps between their expectations and tangible reality. They use what they have been given and create the most with it.

I'm dwelling on the point: Joy lives within the Journey.

In fulfilling the concept of being human, the more you grow, the more you transition into a life of joy.

The more you transition into a life of joy and grow, the more there is of you to give to something greater than you.

> YESTERDAY
> I WAS CLEVER,
> SO I WANTED TO
> CHANGE THE WORLD.
> TODAY
> I AM WISE,
> SO I AM CHANGING
> MYSELF.

VI

PLAYER/COACHING

In *Moment Time*™, as you live your word by fulfilling the mutual commitments, you will, in time, become your new team's Player/Coach. *Joining*, of course, happens first.

The sixth aspect of *Moment Time*™ is *Player/Coaching*, a *process* similar to coaches working with players in training camp and game conditions: Run the play, see what happens, do it again better with each new effort. Feedback loop training creates constant small wins.

Constant small wins build confidence, which lead to you feeling better about your life and your sense of worth.

Bill Russel is the greatest Player/Coach of all time. He honed his skills on the court while leading his teammates to be the best players they could be. Together, he and his teammates, the Boston Celtics, won two NBA World Championships (1968–69). He is a great role model.

Master *Player/Coaching* by practicing coaching. To make this process easier to understand, imagine you just joined my team. You *friend* twelve people your first two weeks (six per week). After each *Friending* moment, you and I review what happened, and determine how you can execute *Friending* better in the weeks ahead.

You invite six of these twelve to meet for a *Clarifying* moment. We review these six experiences. You invite four of these six to a *Trusting* moment. We review these four experiences. You discern which two of the four to invite to *Inviting* conversations. The sequence of *Friending*, *Clarifying*, and *Trusting*, each with a day or two in between, emphasizes that building relationships and trust take time.

Together, we do the one *Inviting* conversation per week, for two weeks, and invite one of those passion-driven, business-savvy people to join your team. He or she joins. Now you are their Player/Coach.

During the next two weeks, I am still your Player/Coach honing your skills as a Player. As we review your Player conversations, I will also coach *you* as you Player/Coach to coach your new team member. You are learning by doing, getting better and better as the days and weeks go by. **As your Player/Coach, I will always be here for you, even after you become unforgettable, infallible, and unstoppable.**

During every two-week cycle, you and your new team members each repeat the process. Heart-centered, passion-driven, business savvy people join your teams.

Industry lore says it takes three to five years to build a significant sustainable income. Why? Seventy percent of new entrants to the industry *never enroll anyone*, and 20% only enroll one or two. People waste years working with the wrong people.

That's why our mantra is, *Team member . . .*

Let *time* be your friend.
Let the *S.Y.S.T.E.M. do its work.*
***You* do your work.**
Meet one person a day.
Discern who qualifies for more conversations.
Practice people-connecting until you can't do it wrong.
Follow the process.
And let the rest take care of itself.
And so it is . . .

> Yesterday is already a Dream
> and Tomorrow is only a Vision;
> but Today well-lived, makes
> every Yesterday a Dream of Happiness
> and every Tomorrow a Vision of Hope.
>
> – SANSKRIT SAYING

VII

UNFORGETTABLE, INFALLIBLE, UNSTOPPABLE

The greatest challenge with creating and living our dreams is that we plan our lives in years, but live our lives in moments.

– Dave Blanchard

We are in the life-changing business.

Our language describes a new paradigm, a new process.

Old network marketing language is that distributors do two things: (1) sell product and (2) enroll others and teach them to do the same thing second. Does this sound like fun?

According to a 2005 Yahoo poll conducted by the Harris organization, 75% of American adults have considered starting their own business. Therefore, there is an abundance of people who would love being in business for themselves if they felt they had a reliable opportunity to succeed and if it sounded *fun*.

Unforgettable. During *Friending*, people act like kids on a playground looking for kids to play with, or they invite the kid down the block to play. Playing is fun. If playing feels good, they ask that person to play again. When they meet the second time, they act like pre-teens enjoying a sleepover, exploring what their lives will be like when they grow up.

Here's the real question. When you play together, do you feel an increased sense of energy? Slow is fast. Less is more. Be gentle and patient. Let yourself feel what *is*.

Unforgettable is the rare person who is impossible to forget. Rareness is achieved by intrinsically validating friends and creating safe places to build friendships. Validating another happens in all moments, not just the first one. Think about it. When did someone validate your intrinsic worth as a human being? Have you felt loved even when no words were spoken? Did you feel safe with them?

If you can remember this person, they are *unforgettable*.

When you "be/do" in a similar way, you too will be unforgettable.

Infallible. People love to win. Wins, no matter how small, flood the reward centers in our brains with happy molecules that evoke joy, happiness, and triumph. We also want to help friends avoid losing, because everyone hates losing. Losing blocks the flow of happy molecules and creates that *ugh* people feel when frustrated, stuck, or overwhelmed. Not having an agenda avoids losing. Not enrolling people likely to quit avoids losing. When friends win, we win.

How do Player/Coaches help Players feel infallible? Reviewing moment conversations and commenting on what went well are wins. As moments happen, validation may take the form of looking for what feels right in the Player's descriptions of moments; for what they enjoyed during the moments and *asking them to say more about it.*

The American College of LifeStyle Medicine encourages its physicians to start patient visits with the question **"What's going well?"** (versus "what's wrong?") to encourage their patients to initiate mindsets that promote emotional well-being. Research shows effects similar to how we described the mirror neuron process in *Friending*. Starting with a positive psychology-based question also improves the physicians' emotional well-being. Results: the patients and the physicians feel happier during the office visits, and patients' health outcomes improve at a statistically significant level.

How do kids learn to walk? Good parents encourage every step taken.

We use the same process. By positively questioning and validating "what went well?" as the first question, both the Player and the Player/Coach start out in a positive mental state. They both feel better, so the results derived from the daily check-in coaching will escalate over time.

Unstoppable. *Moment Time*™ involves eleven winning moments before each *Inviting* conversation. Since you set aside your personal agenda in these winning moments, you can't be rejected. Never!

John Wooten coached UCLA's basketball team to 88 straight victories. Imagine how his players felt. Capture that feeling. Your feeling your 88 wins in eight weeks creates the unstoppability you will feel while implementing the *Moment Time*™ system.

People who use *Player/Coach Marketing* never quit too soon. They do the necessary work because they know they will achieve the blessed state of equanimity.

> Strive not to be a success,
> but rather to be of value.
> — ALBERT EINSTEIN

> Good friends help you
> to find important things
> when you have lost them.
> Your smile, your hope
> and your courage.
> — DOE ZANTAMATA

VIII

MANAGE YOUR FREEDOM EXPECTATIONS

The book opens with two promises: you will enjoy Time & Financial Freedom, and you will enjoy Emotional & Mental Freedom.

Fulfilling the first promise is relatively easy. When you work in the prescribed manner, you will achieve time and financial freedom *if* you can determine how much is "enough" by "when." If you are not willing to determine how much is enough, then no amount is ever enough, and you will never enjoy time and financial freedom.

I work with a medical physician licensed to train acupuncturists. We are designing a seminar he will teach. I have a support role. When I asked what his financial expectations were, he hesitated. I coaxed a bit, and then he more than doubled his answer. We did not get to "by when."

Look back at the *Trusting* chapter (page 16). The seven basics of a business plan are:

1. Goals
2. Strategy
3. Resources
4. Business environment
5. Tactics
6. Personal environment
7. WILL TO WIN

This physician knows I was the first economist for the American Medical Association, and I simultaneously coached 105 large medical groups as a consulting econometrician (financial numbers geek). He trusts me, and I trust him.

My real task is to design our seminars so they meet his financial expectations and mine, too. The seminars will be heavily science-based relative to the efficacy of various nutritional ingredients and how these practitioners can assure their patients are absorbing the recommended ingredients.

Tactically, we will manage the ethical transition from science-based education to utilizing the network marketing model as the strategy for meeting the seminar attendees' and our financial expectations.

There is no one best network marketing company to satisfactorily meet everyone's variations of the seven basic factors stated above.

But there are things I look at first. One, what behaviors does the company reward most, given the nature of its compensation program? Personally, I prefer plans that offer bonuses for team building. Second, I look for uniqueness. Does the product or service have a distinguishing feature that differentiates it on social media? Will it catch attention? Will it sell itself?

Third, what special circumstances exist in the business environment? I'm designing the seminars because my physician friend brought acupuncture to America, set up and opened the first training program in the USA, and authored *Acupuncture in America*, a book describing his experiences. He has a major strategic advantage in his niche.

And fourth, I look at company management. Will the company survive long-term, given who is in charge?

If the four basics I look for are in place, I can Player/Coach anyone who qualifies through the Scouting moments into developing a six-figure annualized income within six to nine months, variations based on how close the chosen company meets the business plan basics.

How can you assure meeting your emotional and mental freedom expectations? Is mastering people connection skills the key that unlocks these freedoms?.

The people you meet while Scouting will enrich your life, as you enrich their lives. Recently, I met a man who effused light and joy. He told me that his father had taught him the "Inner Smile" to cope with his brother dying in a freak accident. I enjoy his friendship and, by the way, his Ola Loa products cleared up a skin condition that was troubling me. *Violà*, my life is enriched.

> "Being a **LEADER** in network marketing — truly being **EFFECTIVE** — means more than just doing things right. Instead it **REQUIRES** that you do **THE RIGHT THINGS**."
>
> – STEVEN R. COVEY
>
> The 7 Habits of Highly Effective Network Marketing Professionals

IX

ONGOING LEARNING

Before you can make money while you are asleep, you have to first learn how to make money while you are awake.

– Marisa Murgatroyd

Action with feedback loops is learning by experience on steroids. By Scouting and Player/Coaching daily, you immerse yourself in ongoing learning. The four options for continuous learning:

1. *Good*: Free Study
2. *Better*: The *Moment Time*™ *Momentum* Memberships
3. *Best*: Build Your Team
4. *Ultimate*: Go Even Deeper

> Tell me and I forget.
> Teach me and I remember.
> Involve me and I learn.

GOOD: FREE STUDY

Study this book.

Let the words sink in.

I held nothing back for this book. My network marketing

team, *Team Moment Time*™, uses this book when transitioning people from *Trusting* moments into *Inviting* moments. Friends absorbing these words accelerates and enhances their comprehension during the *Inviting* moments.

Once a person joins our teams, this book is an initial training guide for their being a talented Player and ultimately a skillful Player/Coach.

BETTER: *MOMENT TIME*™ MOMENTUM MEMBERSHIPS

a. Basic Membership Program:
- Four copies of this book ($60 value)
- Private Facebook Group (a like-minded community)
- Six Zoom-based teaching/Q&A calls; three per month for two months ($74 value)
- Weekly orientation and graduation sessions open to everyone
- A weekly special proactive tax planning Zoom call (value depends on your circumstances).
- Access to the *Moment Time*™ training archive ($500 value)
- Bonuses within the upgrade invitation to the Premium Membership ($114 value)

Total value $748[+++].

The educational impact of the Zoom calls exceeds the content of this book. E.g., during the proactive tax planning call, repeated once a week, we examine the best of the 53 tax law changes that went into effect January 1, 2018, and how these changes increase the value of running a home-based business. The 2018 Tax Cuts & Jobs Act is the first major overhaul of the tax code in 32 years. E.g., imagine hiring any child in your home over the age of six and being able to deduct up to $1,000 per child per month as a business expense, all tax-free to the child. That's just one example. In these bonus Zoom calls, we discuss the top six tax advantages of running a direct sales business out of your home. Ron Mueller, MBA, Ph.D., author of the plain English tax guides I reference on the special Zoom call, asserts, "...tends to save the *average* small or home-based business owner at least $3,500 in taxes, and usually $5,000 or more." **Annually.**

I've been a student of Ron's work for over a decade. His quoted estimates understate the value of your direct sales business if you plan your tax strategies proactively. *By the way, "understates" is truly an understatement.*

The initial investment in the Basic *Moment Time*™ *Momentum* Membership Program is $97 for the first two months; ongoing membership optional $37 per month.

To join the *Moment Time*™ *Momentum* Basic Membership program, please visit **www.MomentTime.com**.

A new membership training sequence begins in each of the first three weeks each month, so hop on now.

b. **Premium Membership (an accelerated Habit Finder quasi-do-it-yourself Program)**

Entry into the Premium Membership is a two-stage process open to Basic Membership members. The first stage is risk-free. You will receive a copy of *Moment Time*™ *Rests on the Habit Finder* in your welcome package. Optionally, you can complete the Habit Finder Profile that measures your 36 thinking habits. Self-interpretation guides will assist in your understanding your results.

When you discern that an upgrade to Premium Membership is in your best interests, you and I will begin our four deep dives into leveraging your habitual thinking strengths, mastering those pesky risky thinking habits that bite you in the butt, and accelerating the growth of your direct sales team.

Ongoing specific benefits include:

- Secret Facebook Group (an elite community)
- Four Habit Finder 1:1 30-minute deep dives ($800 value)
- Og Mandino Leadership Institute Resources ($300 Institute cost)
  - The Habit Finder Practicum
  - *The Greatest Salesman in the World* by Og Mandino
  - *Today I Begin a New Life* by Dave Blanchard
  - *The Observer's Chair* by Dave Blanchard
  - *Equanimity: Conquering Mt. Entrepreneur* by the Institute
- Nine Zoom-based teaching/Q&A calls (three per month for three months; $900 value)

Total value $2,000.

For reference purposes, my private clients invest $6,000 for an individual 15-week Habit Finder program or $10,000 for a 26-week program.

The axiological basis of the Habit Finder is the Hartman Value Profile. It is OSHA-approved, accurate, reliable, and valid regardless of sex, race, religion, socio-economic status, educational level, etc., for scientifically measuring the tendencies and risks in one's habitual functioning in six areas (36 actual habits) that everyone lives in every day.

To begin your risk-free exploration, visit *www.Habit FinderCoach.com/MomentTime*. My personal Habit Finder website will give you access to complete your profile and waive the $99 fee.

You will be asked to rank two lists of 18 items or phrases. There's no self-assessment involved, so you can't fudge the answers, nor will you experience test anxiety. You may encounter some terms or phrases that seem different to you. Just take your time (about 20 minutes) without trying to overthink it.

By taking this action, you have given yourself the rare opportunity to go to a depth of personal understanding that few people ever experience; yet it is here that your success or failure is most highly influenced.

There is no obligation by completing and seeing your Habit Finder Profile. As you view your 36 thinking habit characteristics, ask yourself these questions:

- *What are my natural thinking strengths? How do I think when I am my natural self without pretending or trying to impress anyone or acting out of shame or fear?*
- *How do my thinking habits risk sabotage my income, my relationships, my life?*
- *How do I leverage my unique results?*

Once you opt into the Premium Membership, we'll go over your thinking strengths, including those that are not maximized. We'll look at what unhealthy habits may be blocking you and the pain that this thinking may be causing in your life. We'll look for what we can do together to correct the riskier thought processes, so you may use your mind more constructively. During our personal time together, we can explore any aspects of your personal life, including your health, relationships, and finances. The ultimate goal is to empower you to step out into your world every day feeling comfortable, whole, and complete.

What would that be like for you?

That's where we are headed.

The investment in the Premium Membership is $1,250. The core membership is three months. Thereafter you may join the ongoing Premium Zoom calls as my guest.

New core membership sequences open up the first week of each calendar quarter.

BEST: BUILD YOUR NETWORK MARKETING TEAM

a. Apply *Moment Time*™ in your company of choice.

b. Engage Clifford to assist in #a.

c. Join *Team Moment Time*™ *as my private client.*

Option #a is the DIY – Do It Yourself – pathway.

Option #b engages me to privately coach you and your team in your company of choice. The book, *Moment Time*™ *Rests on the Habit Finder,* outlines group and individual options for private coaching. If private coaching appeals to you individually and/or your team, please contact me directly. My mission is to impact our industry in a meaningful way. I'm all the way open to discussing how you and your team can alter the culture in your company of choice. In essence, we could even co-venture teaching my intellectual property, and teaching the full integration of it with the Habit Finder if you were to become an Og Mandino Leadership Coach. The first step would be to create a basic *Moment Time*™ membership program exclusively for your company, including revising this book with you as the co-author.

In option #c, the highest level is for you to become a private coaching client; I become your Player/Coach *in the company we together choose* and ***your Habit Finder™ Coach*** as discussed in the next chapter. The usual and customary coaching fees are $6,000 for a 15-week coaching program or $10,000 for the 26-week program. When you opt for the 11-payment plan and invest the down payment. I'll meet you half-way. As long as you are investing your best efforts, I'll reimburse $1,000 out of my earnings as a result of our working together and waive 50% of your ongoing payments.

You invest your best efforts. Team Moment Time™ will continue to work with you and support you until your *annualized monthly income* exceeds ten times your financial investment.

Best efforts include:

- Trust and believe in yourself.
- Trust *Moment Time™ Player/Coach Marketing*. Complete the moments and moment reviews.
- Trust the Habit Finder process. Do the exercises.
- Validate friends on their Facebook pages.
- **Have *fun*. Enjoy your journey.**

If investing in private coaching is not financially feasible, and you want to join Team Moment Time™, please contact me directly. We'll determine what types of companies might work well for you, and the company I recommend for you. If it appears that a company I play in would work well for you, we'd look to see if you are referred by a current team member. If so, you would be placed on that team.

Based on your individual circumstances, you may also qualify for a scholarship of the Basic Membership program.

X

ULTIMATE: GO EVEN DEEPER

Go confidently in the directions of your dreams.
Live the life you have imagined.

– Henry David Thoreau

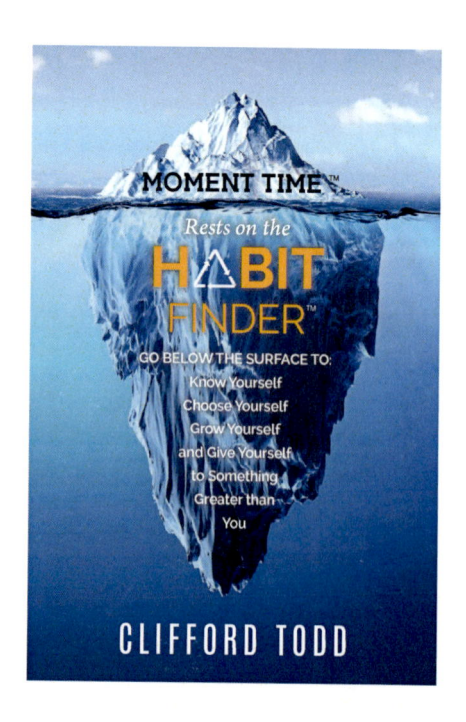

Moment Time™ *Rests on the Habit Finder*™ asserts that these two core thought systems are part of the same ice.

The Habit Finder™ takes you on a journey into your true self where again you explore the core human values:

- Know Yourself
- Choose Yourself
- Grow Yourself
- And Give Yourself to Something Greater than You

I encourage you to explore what makes you authentically you and how you can grow *You* into the best *You* can be. Here's how the Six Moments of *Moment Time*™ line up with the respective Six Habits of the Habit Finder.

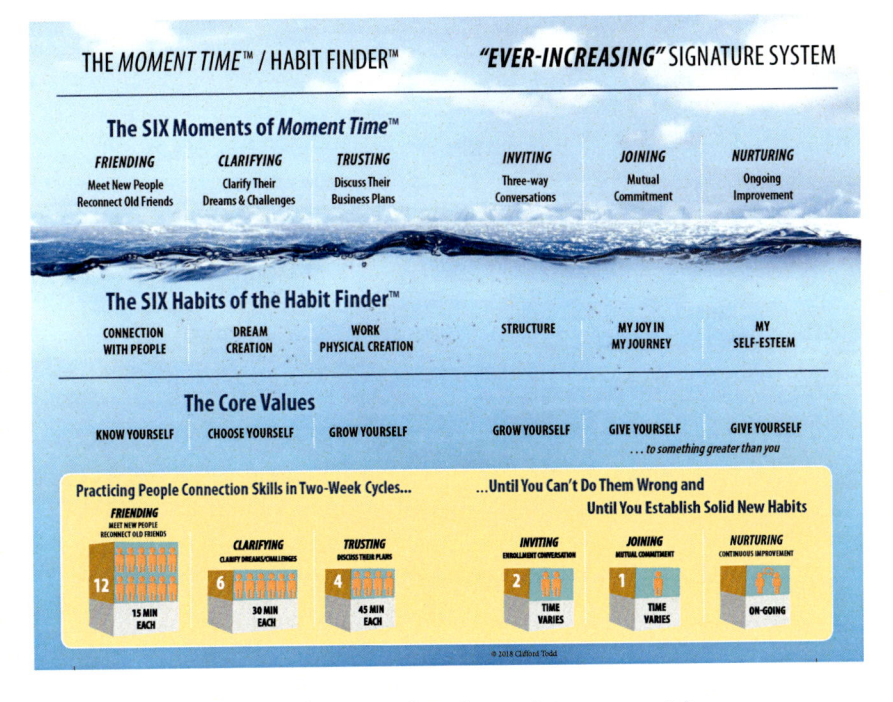

THE *MOMENT TIME*™ / HABIT FINDER™ — "EVER-INCREASING" SIGNATURE SYSTEM

The SIX Moments of *Moment Time*™

FRIENDING	CLARIFYING	TRUSTING	INVITING	JOINING	NURTURING
Meet New People / Reconnect Old Friends	Clarify Their Dreams & Challenges	Discuss Their Business Plans	Three-way Conversations	Mutual Commitment	Ongoing Improvement

The SIX Habits of the Habit Finder™

CONNECTION WITH PEOPLE	DREAM CREATION	WORK PHYSICAL CREATION	STRUCTURE	MY JOY IN MY JOURNEY	MY SELF-ESTEEM

The Core Values

KNOW YOURSELF	CHOOSE YOURSELF	GROW YOURSELF	GROW YOURSELF	GIVE YOURSELF	GIVE YOURSELF ... to something greater than you

Practicing People Connection Skills in Two-Week Cycles... ...**Until You Can't Do Them Wrong and Until You Establish Solid New Habits**

FRIENDING MEET NEW PEOPLE RECONNECT OLD FRIENDS	CLARIFYING CLARIFY DREAMS/CHALLENGES	TRUSTING DISCUSS THEIR PLANS	INVITING ENROLLMENT CONVERSATION	JOINING MUTUAL COMMITMENT	NURTURING CONTINUOUS IMPROVEMENT
12 / 15 MIN EACH	6 / 30 MIN EACH	4 / 45 MIN EACH	2 / TIME VARIES	1 / TIME VARIES	ON-GOING

© 2018 Clifford Todd

And the trouble is, if you don't risk anything, you risk even more.

– Erica Jong

The six habits of the Habit Finder each profile six subcategories of thought:

- **People:** These habits of thinking impact your connection with people.

- **Dream Creation:** These habits of thinking impact your finding, getting clear, and having the motivation to create your dreams.

- **Work:** These habits of thinking impact your focus, effort, and actions—actually doing the work—to complete the tasks and achieve your dreams.

- **Structure:** These habits of thinking impact your discipline and structure—how you think about thinking.

- **Joy In Your Journey:** These habits of thinking impact how you feel about your life.

- **Self-Esteem:** These habits of thinking impact your feelings of self-worth.

During regular 1:1 coaching, I work with clients for an hour per week on multiple areas of concern in their lives. I player/coach their 12 people connection moments each week. The growth I see in clients' lives continues to astonish and delight me.

If private coaching speaks to you, let's review your Habit Finder Profile and lay out what you would like to achieve during the next four to six months.

Results: you will acquire increasing abilities to take on increasing responsibilities with increasing ease. You will achieve results in your relationships, your health, and your finances. You set the agenda and we work together on your journey towards realizing your dreams.

And so it is…

MEET THE AUTHOR, CLIFFORD TODD

Henceforth I will take every risk and embrace every opportunity that may provide a better life for me and my family. I will despise myself later if I look back on my life and realize that I had the talent and the ability to do great things but could not find the courage to try.

– Og Mandino

Dave Blanchard says I am rare. "Clifford is a wonderful human being and a Habit Finder Coach dedicated to making a difference in others' lives."

I have a lifetime of coaching experience. In 1971, I parlayed being an economist for the AMA into coaching medical group administrators, including fifteen Ex-National Presidents of MGMA, the Medical Group Management Association. Its members manage two-thirds of the American physicians in private practice. In the 90s, I trained physicians to introduce wellness protocols in their practices. Today, they call this style of practice Lifestyle Medicine.

I have enjoyed direct sales successes and endured failures. Recognitions like an engraved crystal vase presented on stage (3 awarded; out of 3,000 distributors), best single check $61,234 (2004), longest continuous receipt of checks from a single company (1993–2003), group monthly volume $1,378,000 (1992), certified company trainer (2000), 206 personal customers (1989), along with many failures.

Family history: I was seven years old. My uncle had just died. My grandfather died before I was born. Both were named Clifford Todd. Both men died as a result of medical malpractice. I reached my arms up to my father saying, "It's okay, Dad. I'll fix it." I worked full-time in medical care. My direct sales successes were achieved with part-time efforts.

During 2014 and 2015, I had painful network marketing failures In January 2016, I met a woman who introduced herself: "Hi, I'm Crystal. I work with people who have addictions. What's yours?" I said, "None, unless a bottle of wine a day counts." She embedded a new thought pattern in my mind and worked with me for three weeks. I haven't purchased wine since. This success transformed my "I'll never do this fricken' business again" into my writing a book to reduce the 98% incidence of shattered dreams that the industry inflicts, plus eliminate the rejection people feel when they vomit information on anyone who will listen. Months later, a 110-page draft in hand, I met Dave Blanchard.

Player/Coach Marketing will disrupt direct sales training. My intention is to impact the 98^+% industry failure rate by demonstrating a 90^+% success rate, one person at a time.

We are in the life-changing business. We will impact lives . . . one at a time.

RESOURCES

Clifford Todd
Author, Speaker, Og Mandino Leadership Coach
www.HabitFinderCoach.com/MomentTime
Clifford@MomentTime.com
Facebook.com/CRexTodd
www.linkedin.com/MomentTime
(513) 348-7872

My brother, Hawley, lives in the house where we grew up. When I visit him, he can, *but doesn't*, say "Clifford, go to your room." I've been fortunate to have roots in my life.

I live in Los Angeles, California.

Books available through the Og Mandino Leadership Institute include:
- *The Greatest Salesman in the World* by Og Mandino
- *Today I Begin a New Life* by Dave Blanchard
- *The Observer's Chair* by Dave Blanchard
- *Equanimity: Conquering Mt. Entrepreneur* by the Og Mandino Leadership Institute

My books are available singly on Amazon for $14.97. Multiple copies are available from me: five for $60 [save 20%] or ten for $100 [save 33%], plus shipping.
- *Moment Time™ Rests on The Habit Finder*
- *Moment Time™ Player / Coach Marketing*

POSTSCRIPT

Human Beings are meaning-making machines.

– Jeffrey Van Dyk

When I was 16 years old, I lied on my driver's license and said I was 5' tall. I was only 4'11", the smallest kid in my class, even shorter than all the girls. I had always been the smallest kid *growing **up**?* LOL.

The story I made up was that I didn't deserve as much as the bigger kids, that somehow I was "worth less." So I know what it's like feel unimportant, worthless.

In 1972, I joined Holiday Magic, a network marketing company, to prove the tiny kid wrong. That's what we humans do. We try and try again to prove the stories that we make up about ourselves wrong. Jeffrey taught me this principle.

I kept trying to make network marketing work for twenty years. I would believe the stories from stage, i.e. "I was just a mattress salesman. If I can do it, you can, too." I would allow myself to get sucked in; I'd fail; and I would feel betrayed.

In my 30's, I discovered that my mother, behind my back, years before when I was 23, had convinced Sargent Shriver of the Peace Corps to rescind its invitation to me to train to be a volunteer in Katmandu, Nepal.

So yes, I know what it's like to feel betrayed. I survived by not trusting people.

I suppose I didn't trust God either. Why would He (She?) have made me endure high school gym showers with the body of a ten-year old? Fortunately, entering college, puberty finally kicked in.

Jeffrey, Dave Blanchard and my Og Coach peers helped me understand that our experiences happen "FOR" us, not "TO" us. My journey has brought me perfectly to where I am, and where we are, today.

I too want to be understood.

I want those of you who may have tried network marketing before to be able to create and enjoy time and financial freedom by investing less than five hours per week identifying the one person each week to invite to hear our network marketing story. I want you to feel relaxed investing another five hours per week working on your inner self by being professionally coached. When we work in a company together, you will build new habits and succeed.

Relax again. I gave up deserving less… I will earn awesome long-term income having fun coaching you and celebrating your wins with you. We both win, and so does everyone on our team!

My friend and mentor Eiji Morishita counsels: make your business "fun, easy, profitable, and purposeful."

As far as I'm concerned, it doesn't get any better than this.

This is why the dog is happier!

Made in the USA
Lexington, KY
30 August 2018